W9-CTZ-417

OPEN LETTER TO QUIET LIGHT

OPEN LETTER TO QUIET LIGHT

poems

Francesca Lia Block

Manic D Press

San Francisco

To the friends
who read my poems
during this relationship
and comforted me
when it ended

Open Letter to Quiet Light ©2009 by Francesca Lia Block. All rights reserved.
Published by Manic D Press. For information, contact Manic D Press, PO Box
410804, San Francisco CA 94141   www.manicdpress.com

Cover artwork: *Why Not Have A Happy Heart?* © Irene Hardwicke Olivieri
Printed in the USA

Library of Congress Cataloging-in-Publication Data

Block, Francesca Lia.
  Open letter to quiet light : poems / Francesca Lia Block.
    p. cm.
  ISBN 978-1-933149-30-1 (alk. paper)
  I. Title.
  PS3552.L617O64 2009
  811'.54--dc22
                            2009010727

Contents

pansexual

the satyr found her bathing in a pool
deep at the bottom of a grotto
where she went to lament the broken toxic world

he slipped into the water without a sound
and wrapped his furry legs around her hips
from behind
he whispered with his lips
into her ear
a language she did not understand
pressed his rock
hardness up
against her back
she was not afraid
this was what she had been waiting for
why did it take you so long? she asked him

he rubbed his little beard against her
shoulder
she reached up behind
twisted black curls in her fingertips
tilted back her head
his lips
ragged with lust found her lips
in his rough hands her small exhausted breasts
swelled like honey melons like full moons
then he lifted her
out of the water and carried her to the shore
on his delicate clattering hooves
knelt and thrust into her with the force of his powerful haunches

her body that had once been human
became animals
a brain buzzing like bees
butterfly hands

her heart a beating bird
the cat that purred
between her legs
and then a tiger with a stag
locked in its jaws
who are you? she asked him
and why have you come?

the satyr said a word she did not know
but knew meant *look*
and out of the earth grew plants with powers
to make tumors shrink and disappear
and rain came down
that smelled of the inner depths
of lilies
it washed away the poisons
and on the banks the children danced
their mouths upturned to the sky
and the satyr in his strange language that she now knew said
the meaning of apocalypse my nymph
my nymph my elemental
is only revelation

first date

in spite of what we had lost
our bodies said yes at the first touch
before our minds felt the fear

or did they say yes because of what we had lost?
abandonment takes many forms
but the need for solace
made us brave

we rolled on the floor with the flowers you'd brought
an unspoken question in your hands

you untied my white dress
sucked on my breasts
you reached up inside and discovered me wet
you said *now i can wait because now i know this will be*

let me fuck away the pain
suck away the pain
tuck away the pain
let me flick away the pain
lick away the pain
slick away the pain
let me tease the pain
ease the pain
appease the pain

in spite of what i have been through and maybe because of it
let me tell you this
this
is the best time of my life right now
no one can take that away
this is how
i will always
remember it

mother tongue

speak to me in portuguese she said on their first date
it's such a cliché he grumbled
she asked again two months later and he did it
the words spilling
like water over
her burning
abdomen
as he lifted her
t-shirt slowly up
his lips speaking words first
then another silent language
putting his secrets inside of her

portuguese she thinks
lilting throaty throating lilty
milky silken milken silky
the language he'd used as a child
she tries to imagine him with his round-brown eyes
and curly lashes   his lanky body
it's hard to see him without the goatee   sideburns
but his lips must have been the same
full and brooding

the mother
tongue
she thinks
words and emotions
suddenly one
a part of him she hadn't seen yet
full of tender confidence steadfast longing

if she had a secret language
one he didn't understand
she would speak of babies and his beauty
but she doesn't   she can only moan
and write poetry she doesn't show him

later she cups her young son's face in her hands
it feels smaller and softer than she remembered it
after the bearded large one she'd held no less tenderly
as he whispered his mystery

bleed

i want to bleed and cry on you
from the ducts   from the gash gushing
all my stress and sorrow
but every day i restrain myself
staunch the flow with a tiny white pill
bleed privately on my walks   in yoga   therapy
on the phone to friends
or profusely on the page
the keyboard
forming patterns
peonies and dragons

but when you are inside of me i can't help it
tears and blood spill from my thighs
i only hope that love transforms pain
like poetry

sexualicity

i thought something was wrong with me
for wanting to make love all the time and have six babies
it's only a problem if you don't have someone you adore
to fuck

the doctor who delivered my two asked me if i was done
i made a sound that meant i should be but i'm not
he said *your ovaries are perfect*
and that women my age come to him all the time trying to get pregnant
i told him to shut up
i wanted to call you on the way home and ask you to come over after work
even though we've both decided
sublimation is the way to go

i've had this fantasy since i was a little girl
of an old white house with green trim lots of windows and a terraced garden
i am wearing tight faded jeans a white cotton shirt and high-heeled boots
there is a man working in the other room
sitting at a desk   he works at home like i do
i never see his face but i feel him in my solar plexus
we have many children and feed them outside among the flowers

when you touch me i crackle electric
my veins incandescent
you say you haven't felt that
and i quickly need to explain
that i can experience the same thing when i dance alone
it's not true love or soul mates or anything like that

but i want to plug you in
light you up like a million stars

why am i ashamed of my desire?
isn't it the same as not being able to stop writing stories?
only a problem if you don't have someone to email them to

love/sex/art
that spark of creation
pure beyond shame
just facts
like electricity

seen

people ask me how they look
but i don't see things that way
you say
you took my photo anyway

crowned with purple flowers
smiling fearless in pale blue silk
and sequins
a portrait of my spirit
falling intricately
in love
then   for fun
you carefully
digitally
magically
erased the lines around my eyes

all my sex
fantasies revolve around being seen
stripping off clothes or touching myself in front of you
until I come
dancing
in your spotlight

i'm not sure you're all that interested   though I'm sure you would oblige
you have already seen far beyond the private place between my thighs
the contortions of my orgasm
into my brain with its terraced flowergardens and beautiful dead girls
into my heart with its constellations
babies and winged horses
but would you change them if you could?
digitally enhance them?
remove the threats?

survivor

when my computer stopped working today
it was like somebody took my hands away
cut them right off
leaving the stump of my wrists

without my poetry   my little stories
i am forlorn   hungry and lonely
needing you to comfort me
even the two hundred and thirty-six kissy faces
you emailed me weren't enough

when you called to say you couldn't go
it was too late to dance
not safe walking through venice alone
the parking lot full by then

without undulations to the music
i am needy and tense   legless
just a giant head with a jaw
grinding on the plastic that protects my teeth
from cracking apart in my mouth

what do i need to survive?
two small children
who cry in the night
evening primrose oil and butterflies
songs that make me cry
friends who can listen
tears that glisten
my legs and my hands
but not a man
orchids and platform shoes
not you

you are the one i come to when i am fed
dancing on my dancer's legs
my hands open before me
full of stories

missed

it's hard for me to separate
and stay connected
as if there aren't invisible threads webbing us all
at any given moment

you couldn't come to san francisco
at the airport i saw a man who looked just like you
the black beard   black curls   baggy camo shorts   skateboard shoes
even the hunch of his shoulders in the black t-shirt
he disappeared and i wondered
if he were real
if you were sending me a message of some kind
i'm still here
will be here when you return

how many other messages have i missed?
like your call on my cell
maybe you sent me an electronic kiss
a dream in my vast starched hotel bed
that made me come in my sleep
from the deep place
from the inside
out

did you get my dream?
grilled figs and polenta in the restaurant
on the shiny black water
the gaudi's in barcelona
    that look built by nature and mad elves
    broken mosaic tiles piles
    of fruits and dragons
making love in a tub
of white marble
waking up in a room's
golden bloom

the color of my mother's wedding
dress
in the city we didn't visit
together

growth

you say i'm like a teenager
maybe my development was arrested
when my dad was diagnosed
as if by staying seventeen
i could keep his disease
from progressing

i have separation anxiety
and could dance all night
if you let me
i'm insecure
and wear tight jeans
too much pink and glitter
for a lady my age

i thought i grew up when my children were born
when i got divorced
or at least when I had to put my dog to sleep
but i still feel like a baby
when you have to leave

i went out dancing
to try to get over
this feeling of loss
but even after two hours shaking
my soul in the darkness
i still want to knock on your door

once you said *it's okay you can feel like a baby*
once i called you *baby* when you came

but when i got home alone last night
held my sleeping son's feet in my hands
i could feel the buzz of cells at work
and today when your boy

built me a sculpture from wooden blocks
i could see his eyelashes
growing before my eyes
like baby bird wings
or shooting stars

what i've lost

two cars (stolen)
two cats (euthanasia)
three dogs (euthanasia)
one opportunity to date tall blond bicycle riding bowie listening artist in
    high school (fear)
three serious boyfriends (fear   immaturity   incompatibility)
one pair huge earrings dripping with pink rhinestones (stolen)
one opportunity to live in new york city (fear)
one opportunity to visit and stay with kind sad-eyed writer in brooklyn (fear)
two fetuses (miscarriage)
one husband (divorce)
one diamond ring (ex took it back)
one intricate golden beaded and jeweled cuff from ex (while on date
    with someone else)
one bump of cartilage on previously broken nose (rhinoplasty)
one tall   blond   angelic music making friend (cancer)
one good therapist (scleraderma)
one father (cancer and heart failure)
and
the inability to see that the end is only the beginning

purification ritual

the man said *a time of purification*

every two weeks i have the heavy metals
sucked out of my body
aluminum and mercury and lead
on weekends i salute the sun
until my clothes are soaked with sweat
no tears   though
the tiny white pills make me forget

i've given up alcohol and sweets
dairy   caffeine   meat
chocolate   yeast and wheat
self hatred and starvation
punishment   intoxication
but not masturbation
i tried for three weeks but that was all
and last night
with anticipation
i had a female ejaculation

so don't blame me if i'm disappointed
that i can't see you
the man said not to depend on anyone else
fall in love with the inanimate
but i wanted
the dark sweet slam of your body

instead i walked my dog in the park
the fall day rustled with light
leaves foiled with gold
to press
over the goddess breasts
i noticed the phallic tree roots
enticing a faerie to ride them

at home on the table i prepared for you
the labial lily bud

rock/dragon/light

you are a rock
hard and steady
i am water
rushing over you
gushing over you
licking you
slicking you
teasing you
pleasing you
uneasing you

you are a dragon
and i am the girl at the pet store
looking around in bewilderment
how can i choose the strutting chihuahua
when i know you were curled on my mattress
unfurled on my mattress
slashing and
lashing and
thrashing and
gnashing and
gashing me

you are the quiet light
the kind that intoxicates
the kind that makes it impossible for me
to leave this city
the quiet goldish light of late autumn
late afternoons
the light that i try to capture
before it fades into evening
but it is always gone
i am the night
with my dreams of wolves
my hands in my pants

my heart full of longing and songing
letting and fretting
often regretting
never abetting
sometimes forgetting
that the day comes again

just fine

you deal with the world's fuckedupness by analyzing and planning
i deal with the world's fuckedupness by writing and dancing
and sometimes
by needing you too much
maybe i can learn to think more logically
will you learn to need me just a little?

the soliders look like handsome sooty boys in costume
except for their eyes that are blank-black with death
like the sewer water my son calls *war*
i worry that someone will try to take him away from me
mark him with a star
give him to their gods
i pretend not to wish for you
to protect us take us to
brazil if that ever happened
i pretend then that i am logical already
steady   not needy
just fine

and you know   darling
(may i call you that this once and without obligation?)
i really am
love shines from my fingertips
you told me
tomorrow is the day for positive thoughts
a peaceful planet
star babies   angels
incantations   celebrations
moving pictures in the holy wood
my dream house with the terraced garden
where i feast and dance all night by twinkle light
with my beloveds
like the circle we just made
holding hands and swaying to the beatles

our children's faces alight with love
at that moment
i needed to manifest
nothing more

myths about giving

you can give too much
false: if you feel empty afterwards   it was not really giving

don't give if you feel empty
false: meditate on why you feel empty
fill up just enough to be able to give
you will feel full

both people in a relationship should give equally
false: there is no way to measure giving
both people may give what they can
the one who has more to give in the moment can give more

giving to yourself doesn't count for as much
false: your mother may have taught you how to give to everyone
but herself
give to yourself
then give to everyone as if they were you as a child

love and giving are not the same thing
false: substitute love
above
and you will see

if your lover has a fever
and can't see you and won't communicate with you
and is vague about getting together
pout   go out
grumpily wait for him to get better and call you
false: do yoga   walk the dog
squeeze some fresh vegetables
call your friends   take a bath
touch yourself   read a book
listen to music: cry
call him

offer to bring him soup
send him a poem
love is
for
giving

the end is the beginning

these are the times i died
papa   when you did
john   when we talked about having babies
and broke up that same night
when my skin broke out in cysts
when the fetus's heart stopped beating
when the next one's heart never started
when i realized that the men who were hurting me
were only reflections of my own self hatred

these are the times i have been reborn
a thousand times dancing
with every poem
jasmine   when i saw the round bald crown
of your perfect head
when i first kissed your cheek   my sam
every time you hold me morningstar and michael
when i saw my face   quiet light   in the picture you had taken
when you whispered *2012*
the end is the beginning

faith full

things i know about you:
your name means quiet light
you think before you speak
you don't believe everything you see
you are more curious than fearful
to you death is more mysterious
than fearsome
you are able to cry if necessary
you can enjoy
and not become addicted
your balance is innate
you were loved as a child
and saw a puppy die
you know what you want
you have a tense back
expansive chest
graceful limbs
precise hands
you don't always listen to me
but if i hold your shoulders
look in your eyes and smile
then you will listen
you appreciate a woman's body
but you see her soul
your love for your son is unfathomable
and will always come first
but will allow you to love others
better than before
you are capable of breaking my heart
but if you do
it will not be maliciously or cruel
you believe the universe
is ultimately
a friendly place

things i don't know about you:
what you dream
what you look like when you sleep
your fantasies
(well   maybe one)
how many times your heart has been broken
and repaired
your greatest fear
all the places you have been
where you are going
why it is
that you have more faith than i
how long you will be in my life

this i know   though

why?

contentment vs.

we made you a cake
shaped like a heart
and studded with chocolates
we bought a sunflower bouquet
and a skateboarder t-shirt
i wrote you a poem
because i missed you so much
here you are beside me
playing pin the tail on the donkey
with our kids
licking the salt off your margarita
while the flames from the fire pit
seem to leap from your shoulders
laughing when your son says
you can all have a sleepover at my house
you can sleep in my other bunk bed and
your mom can sleep with my dad!
when we say goodbye
i sneak a kiss into the warm of your neck
and you do too

the trouble
with contentment
is that
i don't want to write any poetry
but i suppose the very fact
that i am looking for trouble
means a poem
shouldn't be far
behind

why i believe in starchildren

you told me about the starchildren
with their three strains of dna
their large heads and large eyes
their efficient lithe bodies
their allergies and sensitivities
how they know more than they should
how they create things beyond their years
here are three of them
sitting across from us
big planet eyes twinkling
long swoony lashes
delicate fingers meticulously
picking at their food
they are quick to tears and kindness
and they read our minds daily
but this is the main reason why
i believe they are not simply from here:
because i found you
when i had finally
learned to love myself
and simultaneously
needed you the most
you with your big brain and compassionate orbs
your dexterity and balance
kind heart   x-ray eyes   and healing hands
with the way the world is these days
it takes a pleiadean
to teach someone how
to be a human

scary time

i worried that when you said
you had different ideas about time
you meant my sense of it felt constricting to you
or maybe i was just threatened
thinking you
committed to the now
might never make a plan
in advance
then you said *audrey hepburn is pretty*
which she is   the prettiest
and we saw a movie about gangrene and endangered
babies and rifles and pain
and the loud sounds made me jump
but i was scared to hold onto you
so i sat there wanting
you to hold me and tell me i was pretty
as if that would soothe me
even though i know
i am supposed to
know i am pretty enough
and safe
and soothe myself
and remember
that things happen when they are supposed to
so then we went home
and made a little shrine
in the back room with sunflowers and candles
and music and quilts and pillows
and made love
and you were so strong this force i could fall
onto backwards and without
looking
and i felt my brain chemistry resetting
all the anxiety leaving my body through your moan
then we even slept for a few hours

in each other's arms
getting used to each other's bodies at rest
and i didn't need you to stay past dawn
or tell me when you would see me again
or even that you loved my body
i just remembered how you said
you would illustrate my poems
with your photographs
and take pictures of me stripping
and you called me *baby* once
touched me more tenderly than you have done before
and that was enough
because that was now
and now was all there was

malled

they got trapped in the mall
a maze without exits
there were no people at work
only speaking machines
there were special stores
designed to make women feel old and ugly
and others to make men feel small and poor
the perfect though headless mannequins
sang a little refrain
what is a flower   a bird with wings?
you can never have
what you really want
the man and woman
stumbled around together
under the lights designed to make them feel weak
the woman's heels were too high
she was afraid she might fall so occasionally
she would grab onto the man's bicep
but then the voices hidden in the walls
told her to keep her hands to herself

because they were stuck here
they decided to see a movie
the movie was about a man who shoots his wife in the head
and rapes his deaf mute daughter
and gives away the rifle
to a man in the middle east
who gives it to his sons
who shoot at a bus
one of the sons dies
his brother may or may not die
the woman shot on the bus
may or may not die
her children may or may not die
her nanny's nephew may or may not die

the deaf mute daughter
may or may not die
the movie boomed and bled all over the screen
the woman kept jumping in her seat
she wanted to grab onto the man the whole time
she wanted to be home with him
making love under a quilt
away from the mall

after the movie the man and the woman
decided to make their escape
so the woman took off her much too expensive shoes
the ones she had bought in another mall
because the mall's walls had told her
she was not pretty or sexy or successful looking enough
without them
and she gave them to a shoeless woman who had somehow
gotten into the mall
and the man seized her hand up in his
in spite of the warning voices
and they sprinted past the mean enticing stores
that beckoned like sirens
and they paid their last money
to the talking polite but mean machines
and as they ran the man told the woman
things about his childhood in brazil
about his mother who looked like elizabeth taylor
when she was young
and about his daredevil brother
and drinking the juice of the cashew fruit
and the magic of skateboards
that are just a plank with four wheels
but can take you anywhere and do amazing things
and the woman didn't tell the man that she was afraid
but kept smiling and listening to him and holding his hand
knowing that later she could put her fear safely in a poem

and that was how they escaped
to a little house overgrown with vines
and filled with sunflowers   music and candles
and they took off their clothes
because they didn't need them anymore
and they made love
and the woman said to the man
if the end of the world is anything like that movie
i hope my children and i are by your side

and the man said
baby   the end of the mall
is only the beginning
of the garden

strategies

i am trying to find ways of dealing
with not knowing when i am going
to see you
so
i think about the movie
i am going to make with my friends
and the new book i am going to write
and my trip to seattle
and yoga and dancing
and my longed-for children
with their love letters
and my friends like sisters
and i think about the nice man
who seemed so familiar
and gave me his number
and asked if i were married
and the not so nice man with the unsettling blue eyes
who wanted to speak to me alone
and asked me if he made me nervous
which he did
but i said no he didn't

i have lots of strategies
to make me feel better
but all i really want to feel is you
crouched behind me
while my face falls
into a bouquet of white lilies

is this desire right
or am i like the girl with sad eyes
who asked me if i got the cd
she made for me
and if i liked it
and when i said *yes* and *thank you*

thank you so much
it was not enough
as nothing could ever
ever
be
enough

black dress

i keep seeing a black dress in my mind
it is satin
thin straps
fitted bodice
and a full ¾ length skirt
the fabric intricately
pleated
to create some kind
of petal effect

the black dress could be so many things
it could be the little black dress
the one every woman should own
according to the fashion magazines
the one that i somehow
have never been able
to get right
wearing an ill fitting skirt and top
or a cheap dress from target
or just a black slip
or white dress instead

or it could be   that haunting thing
a dress of mourning
   it certainly isn't
   long and white
with a small and elegant
cashmere sweater over
it would be appropriate
for a funeral
i really have nothing like that
in my wardrobe
my father was cremated
even though he was jewish
and we spread his ashes

over the pacific at malibu
but actually i
didn't touch them
was too afraid
at the time
only twenty-four
it seems young to me now
though i thought i was supposed to be a grown-up then
i believe i wore white that day in may
   gulls and tar-stained feet
   sky and sea the same goldspun blue
but i don't really remember

or the black dress could be a metaphor for goodbye
   would you like to fuck me in it?
   i know you like me half-dressed
   only half
   exposed
that is (one of the) wonderful things
about poetry
instead of my grief and fear
i can give you an image
a sexy pretty thing
satin and black
as your invisible
pupils

the camera

the camera came to slay the woman
she saw the picture and said *no you are not me*
and the camera laughed wickedly
and replied *no one else will ever know that*
the woman saw herself as a hag of death
with wrinkles and bags and pallor
but she thought   oh no this is not me
i am fashionable
i am nice looking   sexy
i am in love
no the camera laughed
you are only
mistaken
in shock   the woman shed her skin
until beneath
she was completely raw

luckily there was a shaman
(though he was too much the real thing
to ever call himself that)
he had huge bones
and huge eyes
that were cameras also
with which he made visible the souls of people

the woman was too raw to be afraid
the shaman lay her
out on his bed
where she grew a new
skin
he spread her gently but firmly
apart
and read her like a book of poetry
then he illustrated her with his eyes

she looked like she felt inside
she looked like a painting in a museum
with a flower on her head
with a smile and eyes of love
reflecting the huge-boned
camera-eyed
beautiful shaman
who had died at least once
and been reborn with this gift

a long time later
the wicked camera will come to the shaman and the woman
and say *none of what you have done matters*
because whatever you appear to be inside or out
will soon be over
but by this time the woman and the shaman will not care
they will already be busy shedding their skins
simultaneously staying the same
and becoming
something
completely
different

erotic nature

animal
your power haunches
your musky scent and the black hair like fur
i link my arms through and hold on
for the ride

root in the ground
thick and juicy with moisture
buried so deep
into the soil of me

rose petal glittered
with droplets of wetness
striated with shades of pink
you are the hand that plucked me
and i screamed with silent pleasure
like a woman being held from behind
with her face in a pillow

matching bird wings i saw on my walk
i wanted to take them home and study them
the model for an angel
but though perfectly in tact
they were ripped at the source
torn and bloodied
by your teeth

a man and a woman
the light was on this time
the bed unmade when i arrived
i smelled you in the tangled sheets
i cried a little and you said *tears are good*
crying's good
sometimes i cry for happiness
i smiled   i said *stop   you are spoiling it*

how can i be sad?
it is impossible
when every living thing's alive
when i see the bittersweet
cacao of your eyes

core issue

can't breathe
can't swallow
heart pound
stomach shrink
skin shrivel
pain of untouch
i'm going to die
please
come
hold
me
mommy
where are you?
that baby needs a lot of holding my therapist says
that baby needs a lot of holding
holding me with her good voice
i nursed my daughter through the whole night
when she was in the hospital
i was pregnant with her
brother i never
left her side
i am going to die
if you look at that beautiful woman
and you don't hold me
i am going to die if you don't tell me i am pretty
if you don't save my life

my boyfriend is an alien

my boyfriend is an alien
he can read my mind
and has only made me cry
one time
in four months
he does not think i am too wet
nor does my poetry frighten him
(too much)
his eyes are supernaturally huge
his head is big and his bones are heavy
but he glides like skateboarding when he walks
and makes no sound
he speaks a language that sounds like poetry
and sex
he thinks female earthlings
are confusing   emotional and lacking in logic
but he likes us anyway
he thinks *break your heart* means
hurt your feelings
and says he never wants to do that
he has no sense of time
and lives only in the now
which can be pretty annoying
when you are trying to make a date
but is great
when you are making love
and he says that when he came
he was on another planet
and no one else was there
except the two of you

we run into the night
the music gives us chills
he points out the secret messages on the walls
he takes my hand and we fly over the canyons

he reaches inside me
and removes fear
like psychic surgery
on a tumor

fearless
i think i may becoming
alien too

how can you blame me for overflowing into these poems?

what else is there to contain
my love for you after a night like this
eating lotus root   kabocha pumpkin   spinach   and broiled rice balls
at the hole-in-the-wall
your big brooding eyes and shoulders
your delicate hands with the broken wrists
your voice saying energy like *enerjeee*
and electricity like *electrissiteee*
the brave sorrow when you say you met her seven years ago
day before yesterday
at thanksgiving in big bear
where you went to find snow
and found a wife
the mother of your beloved child
the cute girl next door
literally
with big green eyes and big breasts
who knew about computers
and extreme sports like you
and it is so far away and yesterday
and then everything changed so suddenly
leaving your heart smashed like glass
and you said
i need someone to share my loss
and you can cry in my arms any time you want
and you can talk about how she left you
how much you loved her
but my darling
when we lie in your bed
surrounded by dead can dance
on four speakers
and you taste my breasts
like they are the most beautiful
nectar of all
and you reach your hands between my legs

and roll me out of my clothes
and murmur and grumble and groan
and come inside me
where i bleed
and you fall asleep all eyelashes and pouting lips
just like your child
and hold me against the warm expanse
of your beating chest
playing its own song
do not expect
me not to overflow
do not expect me
not to call you darling   lover
and tell you this
i need someone
with whom
to share
my joy

you were late for my party

everyone else was on time
the girls came in their saris and wings
they played music and sang on the lawn
and the jewish hare krishna with the craggy voice
fed me lentils with coconut and ginger
and watched me dance
by the time you arrived
the rose quartz beads were hot as fire
on my neck
you held them in your pocket while i was lifted to the moon
there were bushels of flowers pinkwhite roses lilies gladiolas
wine and sweets
you had driven across town to get me some weed
because i asked you for it
at the last minute
there was also an embroidered sweatshirt in a bag
the goddess girls vanished leaving no trace
the friends left
left their cups of wine their orange peels and their gifts
when everyone was gone
we sat on the step under the moon you said
that everything looked silver
and it was the best party ever
i took too long to decide what music to put on and you laughed
you said *there better be music on*
when i get back from the bathroom
because you were hard already
i sat on top of you and danced moving my arms in the air
like flowers unfurling
you said *that was so beautiful*
you are silhouetted   it's like an angel or a goddess
dancing just for me
stars shot through my womb
after you came you entwined my fingers with yours
you so intricate so dexterous

and my hand came too
you lay in my arms and told me about being
embarrassed as a teenager
even by your thick black
curls that crackle
electric
the weed was why
you were late
there is no bittersweet raw sad way to end this
for the sake of poetry or my anthology
only a word that has lost its numinousity
happiness only

mr. black and the lovely chakra present

i like pink
sex and soul together
color of the dolphin that the indians in brazil
tell of
coming out of the river at night
to make love to the women
succulent and furtive like you

i want to give you all the colors but you have most
red at the your tailbone shade of the source
orange for your pelvis pumping and holding
the seed that made that boy with those eyes
yellow for your solar plexus center of power
indigo mind always at work
violet white light shining spirit

refusing to rely on anyone or admit your need
you almost always wear black

but your green heart was broken darling
and i've never heard your blue throat
sing

time

you don't believe in time
feel the calendar should be changed
to reflect the cycles
of women and the moon
you believe that age is a concept
not a reality
that i am as much seventeen
as forty-four
because that was when my dad got sick
and my heart became an empty vessel
for desire and poetry to fill

the rain fell all night
the room smelled perfumy vanillabean
from white lilies and expensive candles
there were new sheets
i kept some clothes on
a black lace bustier and miniskirt
i was pouring sweat from every pore
and my legs kept shaking
even afterwards
by morning i lay fully naked
curled cleaved
to your warm side
watching you breathe
your eyelashes the bump on your nose your luscious
lips
you reached and put your fingers inside me
sighed to find
me ready
we made love so long
i lost all sense of time
you stayed for coffee
eggs and a blueberry smoothie
you even took a shower and played a cd

didn't run away
hugged me for a long time at the door
in your soft gray sweater
where you had hugged me the night before
and said *i missed you*

later on the freeway
the sky opened like a pale blue
jewel box
full of infinity
the raindrops were sliding up
the windshield
as if time was reversing
and we
we were
only getting
younger

something i shouldn't plead for

if you sleep over
i promise i will brush my teeth before i kiss you
i will wash my armpits in the morning
i will close the door
so you don't hear my doggy
thumping and scratching
i will be available for sex all night
tumbling across the bed
upside down backwards inside out over the
top
but i'll play hard to get if you want it
pretend to be slightly bored and not as into you
as you are into me
or i will lie awake on the other side of the bed
giving you space and rest
not even touching you
just dreaming of fucking you
i will get up and make you breakfast
fig smoothies and waffles and eggs with butter
or I will let you take me out to breakfast at your favorite place
i will buy white roses and white lilies and pink roses for the altar
and light the best sweet creamy vanilla bean
scented candles from my poet girlfriends
and plug in the twinkle lights before you get up

you said you want our relationship
to stay like a perfectly wrapped
present
and not be touched
by the real
world
but did you know
if you never tear the wrapping
you will never see
the gift
inside?

hypergraphia my love

it scratches like a claw
i want you more than any of the things i can't have
ice cream   champagne
beer   drugs
a perfect face
big breasts
movies made of all my books
a house overgrown with white roses
chocolate cake
whipped cream
fifty pairs of prada
shoes
the ability to fly

what do i want more than you?
my children
because without them i would not have a heart
with which to want
poems
because without these words
all my wanting
would eat you
alive

you are still keeping us a secret

i feel invisible
and on display
at the same time
like the ghost of that dog
the one i saw barfing blood
heaving out guts in the middle of fountain avenue
one summer night
on my way to a party
and i just left my body
and didn't register what was happening
until my friend at the party said *didn't you see that dog*
i thought that was you in the next car?
she had gotten out to see if she could help it
but i kept driving in a sick and cowardly trance
and that is how invisible i feel
and how on display
to all the women who know you are dating me
but hiding it   pretending you aren't
and to the ones who have no idea and flip their locks in your face
and wiggle their asses in their jeans
and carry their five hundred dollar louis vuitton purses on their arms
and especially to you when you hardly say *hi* and walk right past
as if i am not the one you pinned to the bed
and fucked from behind
(because you can't come looking into my face)
as if i am the ghost of the dead dog on fountain
both invisible and shining with street lights and blood
the dog
that i didn't stop
to help

she: the haunting

please don't use the condom i don't want to feel any more barriers
between us

she is standing in the corner of the room and waiting
like a creature about to give up her wings

her name ends with ela gabriela daniela raphaela of god
she has thick black curls and eyes so big and dark i could fall into them
and find myself
she has a frida kahlo eyebrow and feathery eyelashes
and full sweet lips like a strawberry
sparks of art fly off of her out of her
there are plays to be performed   dresses to be designed
a daddy once lost who will take her photograph
she knows just why she wants to come

she has been waiting for you   she has been waiting for me   she has
been waiting for us   it is almost too late
maybe she is the baby you had
the one who wanted you to be her daddy so badly
but died right away anyway
you only got to hold her once

perhaps i am delusional
maybe it is just that my love for you has grown so huge
as big as a baby   as big as a child   as big as a returning angel

satisfaction

i will be happy if you give me a sugar
free vegan carrot cake in a pink cake box
and feed it to me with your mouth
i will be happy if you come over in the middle of the night
and climb into my bed and make love to me while i sleep
i will be happy if you buy me flowers again
like you did on our first date
freesia and dahlias   buds wrapped in white netting
i will be happy if you take photographs of me
in rose quartz prayer beads and roses
i will be happy if you sit on my couch and shine a spotlight on me
and let me dance for you to three of my favorite songs
until i am sweating and my blood is pounding
and i will be happy if i can come to you then
and fall at your feet beating and glistening
like a heart
and i will be happy if nothing changes
if we keep dating each other every other saturday
if you never say *i love you beautiful*
if you never get divorced or move in
or give me a ring or take care of my children as your own
and i never have a clitoral orgasm with you present
and you and i just keep doing what we are doing
now
and i would be lying

knocker

there was a door in her chest
at that bony protrusion
that had formed to protect her
from just such things

it was red with a brass knob
a knocker
shaped like a lion
and a peephole at the top
he did not make it
but he reminded her it was there

when it was made
something had to be taken out
some extra blood and flesh perhaps

inside was a land of secrets
terrorists or utopian gardens
i cannot tell you which

when it was reopened
it hurt less than she would have expected
for something carved with a saw
out of bone

what surprised her really
was how much it hurt when it slammed closed again
on that bright
cold noon in december
as she lay unable to come or cry
in her bed
almost six years to the day before the end of the world
as we now know it

the year is dying

like a father with cancer
behind a closed door
like a god with bloody hands and feet
like a goddess losing parts of her body
her dry twig fingers
reaching up into the darkness
as the leaves fall on her grave
and her lover has retreated
into the blackening
sky

let us light a bonfire in the hills of silver
lake eat cake and drink wine
wear fake fur   roses and quartz
my high heeled studded dominatrix
boots
your chocolate
eyes darkening
with lust
while the bohemians discuss
art and sex
addiction
and the apocalypse

this was a pretty good year
i gave up men for half of it
i wrote like a demon
covering first the page then the table
the walls and furniture
the skin on my body
people were impressed but i know
it is a brain disorder called hypergraphia
i danced rarely fearing my soul might be stolen again
when i flung myself around on the hard wooden floor
bruises and wrenched neck

were not as dangerous as dissolution
i became less inflamed with anger
i almost never cried
my children grew
even more
wise and glorious

i found you swimming in a pool
like the giant pink brazilian dolphin
that comes out of the water to fuck women
i found you in an apartment building with a broken front door
hallways full of ghosts   hindu and the smells of curries
a secret room with a high ceiling   candles and music everywhere
i found you in a little muddy preschool yard
building life-sized castles out of plastic cubes
you sat next to me crying while my dog was put to sleep
this year i learned that shaman means
extreme empathy
nothing more
i found you finally in my bed
whispering in portuguese and undressing me like i was a present
that you had wanted forever

this year is dying now
like a father
like a god
like a goddess
like all of us
even the children who we bring forth selfishly
hoping they will help us forget this fact
the year is dying and just like all of us
reborn

the slow vibration of the soul

everything is just a vibration
so what about atoms that vibrate too slowly for us to see?
what does your soul look like
and would i recognize it
if it sped up enough for my sight to understand?
is it more beautiful than your eyes   your injured wrist?

that was the poem i was writing in my head last night
last night i was falling in love with you
across the candles and wine
until you were almost done with the whole bottle
and said drunkenly
what if you were giving birth to a baby
and knew you would die
would you give up your life for it?
and then you said *you can't ask a man this question*
a man would want to save the wife
young pretty beautiful and she can fuck
the kid can't fuck
i would keep the wife
until i met the kid he's the best kid anyone could ever ask for
i wanted to stop you but i only smiled

there is a woman sitting at the table with us
listening as you slur your words
she is young pretty beautiful she can fuck
she is sleeping in my bed between us
under the faded cabbage roses on my quilt
the one feng shui says to get rid of
because it carries the energy of my dissolved marriage
she was at the solstice party
listening to you say *the word boyfriend has a lot of baggage with it*
and examining the wrinkles around my eyes

the woman keeps changing her hairstyles
now she has yarn twisted dreadlocks
there is not an ounce of fat on her body all muscle
i thought her eyes were green but you say blue
she looks like keira knightley
and she is so young
you cover your balls around her
bend slightly as if she has just kicked you in the groin
part of you would take her back any second
even though she left you without a warning
even though if i asked you would say something vague like
i try not to think about the future
or *i would not want to be with someone*
who didn't want to be with me
or *i try to think positive thoughts*
because everything is a vibration

everything is a vibration even my thoughts
even my poems
and every vibration creates a new one around it
i was the one who put that girl in the bed with us
you were only making love to me

everything is just a vibration
so what about atoms that vibrate too slowly for us to see?
what does your soul look like
and would i recognize it
if it sped up enough for my eyes to understand?

snow

i invited you to see the snow with us
but it was fake blasting from a vent above the movie theater
for two songs and then it was over and the night was actually hot
you had promised to come over with gifts on sunday
and it is tuesday and i haven't heard from you
i know you were going to a party and i imagine that maybe you decided
to stay over
so you wouldn't drive drunk
or maybe you decided to go on a road trip with your friends
up to the mountains to find some real snow
that lasts all night and brightens the slope like powdered moon
or maybe your ex-wife had a crisis and needed you on christmas
or maybe your ex-wife decided she was still in love with you
and she and you and your child all drove to the snow together
to make snowmen and snowangels
and you saw her lit up like when you first met her in big bear
she was wearing a tiny white zip-up ski jacket with a fur hood
and her eyes were even bigger and greener in that snowlight
or maybe you hurt yourself and there was an amublance a stretcher
on sunday night i thought to myself i would rather he sleep with
another woman than drive drunk on monday i thought i bet he decided
to go on a road trip with his friends in the middle of the night i worried
you were in an accident this morning i am thinking you are going to
leave me for her and i will leave the mall and put chains on my tires and
get out of my car and roll and roll down the slope gathering layers of
white flakes until i am completely invisible underneath and my friends
will have to scrape me up like ice and shove lexapro in my mouth like
candy and warm my feet by the fire until i melt

poem about fucking trees

i am not interested in those poems about fucking trees
she said and i asked her *what about poems in which you are actually fucking trees*
oh those she said *those i like* and that is what it feels like when you are
inside of me i am a nymph
in the forest and you are tree spirit ragged breathing
like ragged bark the leaves of your hair crisp
and furled in my hands your sturdy trunk
the branches
your
thighs
where
i buck
and
the
root
of
all
life
burying into me

for your mother

she left brazil for new york
young elizabeth taylor
a nanny in a demure dress   hat and gloves
full with the love for two boys she hadn't birthed yet
for your father
she returned
to live on a farm with a bucket shower
and a heater made from a bucket of coal
while manhattan glittered all lights and art
but it was worth it
for your father
for the stars at night the lullaby wind
it was worth it
to birth those boys
see them grow to men
with wise minds pure hearts good hands
i want to take her to the city
to restaurants serving greens   meats and cakes
like the ones she makes so well
i want to buy her flowers
red roses and pink stargazer lilies and white peonies
wrapped in green paper
i want to ask her how she did it
how she made you   raised you   how you became
at least some of who you are
i want to say this to your mother
thank you
thank you for listening to the unborn children
thank you for returning
thank you for coming back

secret place

this is our secret room
dark lit by only one strand
of christmas lights
tossed on the floor
lit by the chants of the
woman in the white
turban and by our laughter
under the covers
here we keep out the loneliness
keep out the cold
the apocalypse
the betrayed man forgets
the girl heals from the cysts on her face
with only the shadow of scars
and no one can come here
not even the we's that we were

do i want too much?

kiss me more
fuck me condomless
speak to me in portuguese
start a magazine with me
take my photograph
listen to everything i say

last night i dreamed you took me up
to the roof to fuck
and look at constellations
they made perfect drawings in the sky
animals and gods
clear and twinkling
as if we were in the desert
with no competing lights

i feels so sad today missing your voice your hands
shivering like my sweet aging mama dog
wanting to sleep in your arms put you whole in my mouth

last night we ate indian food with truth serum spices
and too loud music
and so i said too much
revealed how jealousy feels
like death in my body
how i almost died as a baby
how i'm not a fairy
with a magic wand
but an angry wife sometimes
irrationally jealous of women
with huge breasts brown skin
my hormones unbalanced from four pregnancies in five years
and two of them missed

today i need to tell you i love you

even if it means i push you away a little   forgive me
i can't hold it in any longer
you don't have to say anything back
you have already shown me the stars in a dream love
magical riders traversing the universe
and your voice rich as curry   spicy with truth
telling me not to worry baby
it is all okay with us
it is all
good

fairy tale

once there was a man and a woman
the woman loved the man more
and she made a wish
that she could be for him
all the women he had wanted and never had
or had and lost
and her fairy godmother
(who was a big woman with white hair and a purple caftan
and far-seeing eyes)
came to her and said
are you sure?
and she said *yes i am sure*
and so the wish was granted
so one night the woman came to him
as the most popular girl in his high school
with hair to her hips
and the gait of a cat
who smoked behind the handball courts
and who he had tried to woo
by asking if she needed a light
from his cigarette
but it was the first one he had ever smoked
and it made him convulse with coughs
and embarrassment
and one night the woman came to him
as the model he had photographed
with the face that was
the perfect empty space
to fill with projections
of tireless sex
and baked cakes
and backrubs and blowjobs
and one night the woman came to him
as the ex-wife who had broken his heart
with her dimples and her gravelly laugh

and her eyes that still made his heart feel like crushed glass
because they reminded him
of his beloved son
and her small hard body
and her mind
like a little ship strung with blinking lights
moving away into the black
water
but after the woman had slept with the man
in all these guises
he wrote her an email that said
  i finally figured you out
  you are a fairy and everyone you touch
  with the magic gold dust of your love
  is enlightened and changed
and after this
the woman no longer had to be anyone
except herself
and as a reward for what they had learned
the man and the woman
got to live long healthy lives
and produce works of art that then earned them
enough money to buy houses overgrown with roses
and japanese food and cotton sweatshirts with cool logos
and skater shoes and platforms
and trips to egypt to see the pyramids
and to hawaii to see the volcanoes
and to india and bali and tibet
and europe   barcelona and crete and venice
and have giant parties with their friends in gardens
and dance to live music on the lawns
and see their children flourish
grow up and marry and have babies
and the man and the woman
got to die simultaneously
while making love
to the person they loved the most

for your son

she only left because she loved you both too much
your eyes made up of a thousand different greens and browns
half hers your sweet
wise mind and voice
but it wasn't your fault
that love scared her
it wasn't her fault either

she would give her life for you
but not in the way she was once willing to give her life
now you are the reason for her to stay here
and so she stays now
half the time

she is more beautiful than i am younger smarter
a musician i can't play anything
except the floor
and with my feet
a better athlete she does triathlons she is stronger
her body and her hands that can give massages
i can't give massages
i can only write poetry and do yoga and dance
and love and love and love

i will never try to compete with her
if you ever need me i am here though
but i think you only need me
to stay quietly in the background
holding your daddy loving him and helping him to feel
relaxed and safe
knowing that i will never leave him looking
for anything better
he is better than anything
i am not afraid of love now
i hold it to my breast

a voracious baby that might bite
or worse kill me by its departure
but i will never leave

what i wanted

last night you gave me what i've always wanted
last night when i was sorrowful you whispered
may i photograph you?
and i got to be the muse
reclined in a candlelit room glowing with an aura of sunset in the
desert while your camera explored the curves of my body turning me
into something no longer simply human but like mountains mineral
elemental almost immortal
so it makes perfect sense in a way with the logic of fear that i began to
tally up all the things i didn't get
how my tears bewildered you and when i left you didn't walk me to
my car but watched me from my window shining a flashlight to let me
know you were still there

but muses and mountains my love they do not want

what i look like

my spirit knew you before but luckily she has forgotten
so she can discover you all over again
my spirit's eyes if she had eyes would be like jade with the sun shining
    through
my spirit's hair if she had hair would be like ocean waves unfurled on
    the sand
my spirit's skin if she had skin would flush with the rose petalled
    afterglow of love
my spirit's breasts if she had breasts would swell and fill heavy with the
    milk of love
my spirit's hips if she had hips would look like mine
my spirit's wings if she had wings would tremble at her shoulders
    orgasmic when you kiss her
my spirit if she had a body with which to dance would dance on a lotus
    flower
like a blue goddess with a hundred arms
a goddess in a strip club she would sit in your lap and feed you french
    champagne
with her mouth and undulate and press your head down and fix your
    lips to her nipples and writhe against your hardness and clench you
    until you flowed into her
but i don't have to tell you this   you see her   you feel her
and you hold her just as tenderly in the body she has now

the day turned glorious i love your face

at dawn the fire alarm battery shorted out
my dog ran frightened to the glass door and cut her nose
there was blood on the green rose rug
my children were with their father for a second night
i missed their warm little bodies growing more beautiful bigger with sleep
my neck wrenched hard with pain
and the rain came down

in brazil where you come from it is carnaval but here the streets are quiet
bankers postal workers and students celebrating dead presidents
no poverty stricken men and women dressed once a year in feathers and gold
like gods
no movie stars flashing their bare shaven bodies under miniskirts
no hypnotic drums
days of partying grease and ashes
people who know that breasts and butts   cocks and pussies
are just body parts
like brains and hearts
just more visible

yesterday on your balcony we smelled the sea and other nights we saw
the moon there
above the rental car lots and supermarket
i had brought you shiny red paper   cut out valentine hearts   dark
chocolate in red foil
condoms in silver and a poem decorated with stars and planets
you removed my silk blouse my studded belt my white jeans and fucked me
like you always do   fierce and kind

by noon today the day turned spangled
blue billows and no tears
my children would be arriving soon
i knew i would make love with you again some time
maybe later than i wanted but you had told me not to worry
and you kissed me as a reminder in the dark underground parking lot
even that place i have come to cherish

we laugh so hard it hurts and forget the pain in our teeth
our stomachs   most of all that old pain in our hearts
so easily reactivated by a word   a glimpse of someone we once loved
the rain stops   it always does   the grass greens nourished
in brazil they are still dancing down the streets
bare breasts painted silver
men shaking their asses
booze and music
maybe some day i'll go there with you

i love your face
the day turned
glorious

i want to take you to the japanese restaurant overlooking the city

enmesh myself in silver netting ensnaring jewels like lights
we can watch magicians at the magic castle
we can eat with our fingers and see belly dancers at a moroccan palace
i'll even try not to flinch when they beckon you to dance with them

i want to be art students in san francisco
taking endless photos of each other
eating cream puff pastries
lounging in bed with our pet chinchilla
getting your name tattooed on my hipbone
sketching us entwined with roses
wrapped in swans
nuzzled in packs of wolves

i want to attend endless birthday parties
where we bounce in the bouncer and slide the slide
until we are giddy
faces painted cake on our fingers goodybags filled with dragons

i want to rub your back with lavender oil
take away your headaches
buy you baggy cream colored wide-wale cords
bring you movies and take out food
french champagne and organic cookies from brazil
have you photograph my striptease
spread my legs for your camera
do anything you ask in bed

how fine to want so much
and still be so content

opposites

what did you do to me?
where did we go?
you were a shadow
sweet smoky black as burned
rose petals
night tendrils your curls
grabbing my fingers
your fingers inside then more of you
breaking me up into pinpoints of light
pixilated static vibrating a million whirring wings
you still and quiet merciless
while i bucked and wailed
the back of you cold
i tried to warm
the width of your shoulders
the thick of your haunches
there was too much of you
my hands felt small and inadequate
but the part that touched me
was slick and hard with heat
wanting exactly what i want
though she's a taboo
we won't even speak of her

parts

my mother brought me into this world so i could find you
for many years i wept to her *where are they?*
only she understood the hole in my heart
she had known it too
lucky that i had her or the loneliness might have won before we met

two babies slipped away at six weeks each
and because i had already danced on galaxies with them
i fell to the ground as if disemboweled
and because i had already danced on galaxies with them
i survived and tried again

the girl was first born with pieces of the blue still in her eyes
her fingers curling around me with remembering
yes yes you are mine!
and yes we have so much to do
dances birthdays books and gardens
but first let us spend a year nursing on the futon
and watching tv shows about babies being born
because this love this reunion is too much to bear
while doing other things

then my boy arrived
nestling into me as if we were one
drinking me i lost myself inside him
now grateful for his jet fighters and war games
because they remind me that he is separate this time
i cannot suffocate him
he has explained it all
mommy we are made
of an exploding star

and then you came
with your boy beloved
another missing part of me

and then you came
with your sorrow weighing down your shoulders and blackening your irises
making you mute   breaking parts of your bones
with your boy and your sorrow making you even richer and more
beautiful

the gratitude thundered through
orgasmic   bright
as an electrical storm
the relief let me finally
sleep
like a woman nearing the last five years of ovulation
who has not been made love to properly before

there is one still left   a girl
i miss her but the other four have made me whole
maybe that is what
she was waiting for

organic roses

the stick bugs really look like twigs
they amble in their glass box seeking rose petals
we can't find organic ones   everything is sprayed

i spilled lori's red wine on my apricot velvet dress
she makes girls out of butterfly wings
said she would splash some more wine
so it would seem intentional
a tie dye bacchanal
blood splashing down my legs
wine like lost babies

tori in the photo
has blood on her legs too
i saw it just that day
i may get to be with her in rome
but the faerie queen cannot be rushed
into decisions

giovanni wrote to tell me he was trying to arrange it
online   i just saw a fragment of his face
pale and round like a moon with funky black rimmed glasses
shaved head and tattoos
he wrote a book about a girl who has my name
and another with a pink cover
lipstick kiss in the corner
he seems to understand me well

your wife shaved her head again
she looks sculptural   a nefertiti
we avoid each other at the preschool
like opposing magnets
and i taste the tang of metal on my tongue

you are remote once more
while blood drips out of me and i seek

petals without poison
but the sticks are dead already
dreaming of rome   tori   another baby missed
in every moment there's a poem
not to catch and share each one
this is loneliness

i rest my case

see it is true life is this good
everything as it is meant to be
this is how i know
i found you
in the darkest breathless place i found you
your eyes were kind your mouth was lush
you said *see see things are as they are meant to be*
you touched my breast you slid me open you drowned inside
the dark grew eyes fireflies
like personifications of our heat
the wounded bandaged heart was unwrapped
a present held out and placed back where it belonged
it began to beat then again slowly
resuscitated
not like those limbless cpr dummies i breathed into
and pummeled with my clasped hands
you see my darling one
true love   the babies and angels
in one form or another
they always come back

what you need to know

a woman (this woman) wants to be told she is pretty
especially when you call any other woman pretty
especially your wife
it would be nice if you could say the word beautiful too

a woman (this woman) wants you to call her the next day
especially if the last thing you say
before you leave is
i'll call you tomorrow

a woman (this woman) wants you to bring her to orgasm first
sometimes
don't worry
she will still enjoy every single thing that comes afterward
(maybe more)

a woman (this woman)
does not need you to fix things
even though she loves you for wanting to
she just needs you to listen with your heart

she does not want you to pull away when she tells you
what she wants
or to change anything about your true self
or to be perfect
even though there are many ways and many times
in which you have been entirely perfect

a woman (this woman)
will still love you
even if you never learn any of these things
she is grateful
for the way you let the other single women at the party
know you are with her
for the way you always kiss her when you make love

for the way you make eye contact
and take her photograph
and compliment her shoes
and say *better now* when she asks how you are
she is devoted
she fell to her knees with tears
running down her face and prayed out loud
to be able to handle everything that comes with you
because you are worth everything
and because she knows without you
her heart would break more than it has ever been
broken before

a woman (this woman)
is grateful to you for reading these words
and she will try to give you your space and your time
let you heal your heart at your own pace
spare you her mood swings whenever possible

this is also true: as sad and dissatisfied as she may sound
she knows you are a good man
she knows
that there are as many things about you
she needs
to learn

bad

the grief would not be eased
with relief
unlike the other ones
jim
mike
pete
fred
quiet light   even your name sounds strange
next to theirs
like a poem in a textbook
that someone ripped out and threw away
there would be no relief
just pure grief
worse than even when my daddy died
because there was cancer and relief when that was done
and the chance for me to have a life and fall in love
but without you there will be constant comeless masturbation
there will be food without taste
there will be teeth grinding away at plastic in the night
fat horse pill sized antidepressants
and tiny sweet sleeping pills
sex and love addicts anonymous meetings
botox and restylane freezing and puffing my face
there will be me yelling at my children
and crying in public
and bad overwritten poems that end without hope
and apocalypse without rebirth or revelation

consecration

i want to give you photographs of all the women in the korean spa the
tall skinny girl with long hair and impossibly upturned breasts the long
girl beside me on the massage table with the high mound of curly pelvis
and on my other side the curvy shiny-skinned girl the women bent
over on stools while other women wash their hair with buckets and the
women slumped and sweating in the sauna and the women walking
upright fully naked asses working so feet won't slide on the slippery
ground the masseuses in black lace bra and panties and me lying here
being scrubbed from head to toe legs apart loofah up even between
my thighs ass spread breasts exposed belly dissolving under the weight
of the woman's hands blood flow increased between my legs for you
and mostly all the fear and sorrow of our argument sloughed off like
dead skin like toxins until all that is left of me is my essence sage vanilla
lavender and lily of the valley frankincense and myrrh woodsmoke
pearl and jade and later when i tell you about all the women's bodies
and you smile and you touch me with your alchemist's hands and finally
say *you are beautiful you are an ethereal beauty* there is no fear in me only pure
gold and my essence only love

phoenix

this is what transforms:

we touch

bodies revealing secret parts
dragon tails and horns and fur
wings and scales and seas
uncurling slippery sliding
over and under and into each other
griffin unicorn mermaid satyr
i become you i become beautiful
faerie
i become wild i become loud moaning free
unfettered endlessly wet and loving
tireless endlessly shuddering
i become lilies staining your fingers with my pollen
white magick witch straining the seams of your jeans
inflamed oracle riding the dawn stained waves of your ferocity
you become you you become me
steady steady stronger
extreme athlete
love scholar
philosopher
expanding like the man made of stars
a giant constellation
rings of fire water serpent
quantum physicist
alchemical phoenix

you do not have to say *i love you*
you do not have to say anything

we have been
transformed
we have become
at last
our selves

easter

while you were fucking away my sorrow
the easter bunny left a basket at the door
shiny green grass wooden toys and chocolate eggs
rhinonculus freesia and larkspur
this rabbit was once a bird
on the verge of death
but the goddess of spring transformed him
into an egg-laying mammal
he is ninety years old
from austria and always writes with a dark green pen
thick accent sweet sparkling blue eyes
his wife is petite and beautiful at eighty-seven
they escaped the nazis and came to america
to live in a mossy grotto in nichols canyon
i once wanted to marry their bunny son
a sweet and grumpy filmmaker
who thought he was a unicorn
he took me out for martinis but never kissed me
now his parents are still hopping around the damp gardens
with lavish spring baskets
you found it when you left
and came back in to set it on the bed
where moments before you had me once again
resurrected

every artist needs a muse

if you were able to write me a love poem
you would talk about how i glow after you touch me
how i get wet the second i see you
not afraid to scream when you're inside me
you would write about my available ass the taste of my breasts
the way i shower you
with food and flowers
beer and kisses
little gifts throughout the seasons
poetry and fairy wisdom
my heart that needs you
the way you keep trying
not to need
me

if i were able to take your photograph
everyone would know the swoon of your lips
before a kiss
the smoldering gaze under bristling brows
surprisingly small hands fierce haunches broad expanse
of chest for your big heart
the tense wordless beauty
of the place where our torsos conjoin
the way your body needs me
the way i keep trying
not to need
you

of the lake

she stands thigh high in dark
water has the same effect as silk
stockings defining her elevated
ass her black hair licks
the small of her back her wings
are labial moist
she will come
up the beach and lie with you shave
your cheeks smooth her
body on yours put you in
side until you cry
out
i am not jealous
i have sent her to you in my stead
she is fearless
able to fly away at any moment
she is without need
she can pretend but does not want
your child

it almost feels like cheating to write a poem about last night because it was a poem already

the way you kissed me at the door like fucking so we almost never left
the house
the way we found the art galleries hidden on the cul de sac
the upstairs all white filled with paintings of eggs and faces
women's sculpted bodies and that one white horse running
like a message from my dead father
   this is where you are supposed to be
   here with this man
   these others the wine the light the chocolate raspberry cakes
   dressed in rosy sparkles talking about traveling to europe
   about books and jewelry and punk music from the '80s film and food
   and soccer
   laughing   flirting with your lover and your friends

and then the party moves to a gallery full of wonder boxes
superheroes magic carnivals ancient egypt ballerinas rocket ships
where you drink more wine and charm everyone
with your kindness and your ravishing hair and portuguese
your mind bright and dazzling enticing as a box of wonder

we eat japanese food at our favorite little place
the dishes of lotus and sesame spinach and pumpkin
and i learn again that i can tell you anything

at home we light as many candles as we can find
and i read the poem for your camera
you shoot me up close focused on my lips my downcast lids
the soft glow light you created the casual ease of your art

and then at last upon my bed
the candlelight is like your eyes twinkling blackness
i cry out *this is too much too much* flowing over
but you are still and calm rock steady
until you too turn to sea

i sit up and say brightly *how do you say*
i love you
in portuguese
and you say it
and i say *see you said it!*
and you laugh and laugh
that was a good trick you say
you stay all night
and once we both wake and hear
the rain on the windows
like a benediction
dancing with our joy

i do not want to write another poem about cancer

about john yu's once six foot ice hockey fit
body diminishing behind the ever expanding lenses of his glasses
or how his daughters and his wife still smile for the camera
still pretty still winning swim meets and making purses out of old kimonos
the little one still going to preschool every day
i do not want to write about john yu's mysterious lung cancer
though he never smoked and always exercised
or about how he can no longer design buildings though he has won
    awards for that
how he can no longer travel around the world as he once did
about the chemo and the radiation and now the brain
cancer

i want to write instead a poem about my lover
how deep and heavy he sleeps bear-like
how i wake in the night to stare at the shape of his ear
the perfectly shaved beard and sideburns
the string around his neck with the pendant i gave him
the white scar on his wrist where they had to pin him back together
after the skateboard accident after she left
before i found him   before he started to heal

i do not want to write about john yu's wife
and how once she too stared at her beloved in the night
admired his hands his long legs his long black hair now gone
dreamed of having his child and then did two times

john yu scares us because he reminds us of ourselves
the potential for illness the inevitability of death
how we are going to have to say goodbye to our sports our work our bodies
our loves our darling ones
but what about john yu's bravery
his nobility his love
does that remind us of ourselves?
when john yu ascends and the pain is gone

and he can go back just as bravely and lovingly to his floor plan
his models his itinerary his game his truth
will we remind john yu of himself?

east side

silverlake hipsters must be young and tattooed
goth haired starlet faced cleavage
laughing and talking over their drinks while i'm on stage
before them i am old   thin   sentimental
reading poetry about fauns and fairies
babies and mortality
cancer and true love
my friends are quieter   they don't wolf whistle when i'm through
sipping french vanilla vodka
might as well be absinthe for this compromised body
men eye me nervously from the bar stools
my black thong is showing above my black skinny-jeans
and i have on the studded belt you gave me
the one to replace the one that tore the first time we made love
but next time i will gird my loins
even better for this part of town
remember to read about blow jobs and nitrous
like that pixie in a silver mini dress and maribou wings
well joan didion is like a hundred my thirty-year-old friend says
and she's god
though they made that horrible caricature of her on the cover of the la times
no woman   even god   wants to see herself portrayed like that
anyway none of this matters
i arrived in a limo in my studded platform pradas
beautiful girls kissed me
told me i too was beautiful
and best of all you sat at the foot of the stage
and wept

black watch

will it tell you what happened after you left
it on my bedside table
how i strapped it to my thin
wrist at the tightest hole
wore it to yoga?
will it tell you that i balanced
inversions without the wall
took it off and put it over my heart
during corpse pose at the end?
your black watch watched
me eat my lunch alone in the hare krishna temple
mung beans and rice and salad with sunflower dressing
by the statue of a blue god in beads
it beeped twelve times at noon
that was its only betrayal of anything about you
carried no scent or other clue
will it be so protective then of me?
your watch was there as i marketed for kale and organic cheese sticks
millet and tahini
apples and beets and ginger
while i got that b vitamin shot at my doctor's office
and walked my dog three times around the park
your watch would not have much to report
until that same dog had a second seizure
staggering and shaking   peeing on the floor
then barking wildly for an hour
while three little children waited outside the closed door
and i couldn't stop crying on the phone with the vet
also this
i'll confess
before i give it back
and it whispers my secret
through your pulse point
into your blood
once in despair and need

i kissed
the face
of your black watch

by the ice sculptures and swirling

chocolate fountain
under the gibbous moon
we attract invitations to our dream
destinations brazil and new york
open wine bar and our best
friends climbing the stairs at the exact same moment we arrive

with you i have everything i need
so more things come
drawn to us like dancing
moths   i'm the candle   you're the match
without you i'm inanimate wax
but you always bear
the potential for flame

even the snotty narcissist in french shoes with triangular heels
immobile face telling me that hats are important
keeping the sun off her lineless skin
ignoring me entirely saying *book people have no style*
i'm a style person she says eyeing the cheap shoes around her
she would grimace if her muscles were still able to move that way
but even the snotty narcissist in french shoes
cannot spoil my night
it would be fun to manifest nine hundred dollar heels or a book prize
a panel with the modern mythologists i so admire
but none of it really matters

it took forty years of dreaming
i have you

crone

she hides inside of me
loose wrinkled skin and old hollow eyes
she has been there since i was born
sprouts hair from warts and gnaws up bones
splinters them and licks marrow for dessert
her breasts loose sacks her belly sagging
back hunched like a tortoise shell
i try to keep her a secret
especially from my easily terrified
lover
who captures only beauty in his camera
photoshops out the wrinkles   whitens teeth
who married a woman ten years younger
so as not to have such a disturbing encounter

he must love me a lot
two years older
to take this risk

i must learn to love her a lot
in order to stay with him

desire

the man and the woman wandered into a video store named desire
a hole in the wall with a gated window
and stacks of movies jammed into a tiny space
in the back was the porn
and the man and the woman went there to look
the man found the ass section
and the woman laughed with him
but that was before all the women on the video boxes started talking to her
hey bitch this guy you're with
we get him hard
he wouldn't say no
there was a woman with come all over her face and others with
ballooning tits and uptilted asses
all of them had blank cold eyes and long hair
and all of them were young
and one of them
the one with the come all over her face said
you wanted a baby too don't you?
another one   you greedy bitch
you want his daughter because you are hungry
for tiny hands and feet and suckling mouths
and unconditionally needy love
you want to keep him forever and you think that would do it
you want to show his ex-wife
the one who is still officially married to him
that just because you cannot get away with shaving your head
like she can with her pretty unlined dimpled face
that just because you are incapable of stirring up in him
homicidal jealousy as she did
you (like her) are a woman
you (like her) can have a baby with your boyfriend
but she is thirteen fucking years younger than you are
and her baby is in no danger of down's
like yours would be
so get the fuck out of my store

and go home and suck his dick
but don't be surprised when before he sticks it in
he meticulously

    here the woman had to admit she was surprised and impressed with
    the porn boxes choice of words

rolls the rubber on

the man and the women went home and had really hot sex
and the woman did not cry or tell the man what the porn stars had said
she did not tell him about the baby she wanted
because she had already mentioned it and almost lost him that way
and in the morning she got up and wrote a poem about it
because that was all she could do to fucking shut
the porn stars up

this girl she was in love with a satyr

he smelled like good bread and the red
wine he drank and spilled
on her shirred
silk velvet dress
he could do the cha cha cha and samba on his small clicking hooves
he could even ride a skateboard
he had furry ears and a furry ass
curly horns hiding in his curly black hair
an ever ready penis
that he liked to bury into all parts of this happy girl
he was fierce sometimes and scowled at her
he had one eyebrow and a goatee aptly named
when he was angry he got quiet
and wore his sunglasses so she could not see his eyes

but the thing was this girl never was really afraid of him
even though technically a man who is half goat is a monster
still this monster was much sweeter than all of the hornless men she had
   known
with their hairless asses and soft feet

this monster's best satyr friend had committed suicide
his true love had left him without warning
his baby had died in his arms
and these things had awakened him and made him human

the girl's father had died of cancer
she had lost two fetuses
and a husband
and these things had made her so sad that she felt like a monster

the girl and her satyr
they were the perfect pair

porn

please please stay inside of me while i touch my clit
even if it takes a long time because of these fucking
antidepressants
please stay facing me with your eyes open
touch my breasts
look in my eyes
don't be afraid
talk to me a little
please let me come this way from the outside in
then you can do anything you want with me
i will suck your cock all night
and i will let you fuck me from behind as deep as you want
you can't tire me out
i'll be your sex slave
i'll do anything
just let me touch myself while you look in my eyes
and i won't even ask you
not to wear the condom
and give me the daughter who is crying for us

i think for the first time now
after seeing you lying there so open
shiny with soft lights and our wetness
that the invention of sex
was a way to deal with the overwhelming
almost otherwise incapacitating
feelings of love
(the kind that make my whole body
pound like a heart)
rather than that love was invented
to ensure we would have sex

if this is true
than love is surely as crucial
to our survival as a people
as a planet
as procreation

nurture

he grew up on a farm washed in a bucket played in the dirt with
chickens and so when it was time to move back to the city he and his
brother were the poor little country boys and people laughed this did
not only wound him it made him guarded so that now he walks with his
shoulders hunched and he keeps his eyes hidden when he doesn't feel
safe it made him resourceful so that he knows how to figure things out
by himself fix the plumbing fix the car the computer it made him able
to adapt to almost any situation soft spoken and friendly and clear so
that now he can be around anyone gracefully and it made him insecure
so that he doubted for years if he deserved to live in an apartment
building without a broken door weeds in the yard it made him an artist
hiding behind his camera and showing the world the beauty he saw in
all things that moved and breathed and danced it made him an outsider
punk rock skateboard culture d.i.y. zines and a tattoo of a scorpion
on his leg it made him afraid it made him strong it made him lonely it
made him flexible it made him blind to the illness of a beautiful young
woman because of her dimples her big breasts her perfect ass her green
eyes and then finally after she had broken him almost killed him like
that puppy in the tool shed it allowed him to see the wounded strong
fearful tender poetry of me

trust and lust

one was sleeping with other girls while he pretended to wait for me
one fucked me once and then was gone for ten years
one didn't do anything wrong he just let me go
one slept with a german woman when i went back to l.a.
one told me he was glad he was less attracted to me
than to other women because i was less of a distraction
one said i don't feel that lower chakra thing for you
after lying next to me naked in my bed for a few nights
one told me his 30 year old ex was the love of his life
and he would never love anyone that way again

by the time you came along it is a wonder i was not dressed
in armor living in a fortress
it is a wonder i let you touch me at all
let alone speak to me

was it something in the opening spell of your voice? your eyes?
the way you lifted your son aloft and kissed him with your brooding
lips? was it just pure animal attraction
lust combined with blind luck? the law of chance?

or is it this—
finally after all these years of work toward consciousness
i can at last trust
myself

goodmorning

something is blooming in my cup a green blossom with an arch of
pearls and my daughter's name also last night we drank wine from
portugal flavored with violets and leather you said you had a crush on
angelina jolie and lindsey lohan angelina okay i mean who doesn't?
not only her devastating beauty but her tough suffering and expansive
bold nature a gorgeous punk rock mama diplomat but lindsey makes
me feel jealous sick and old i won't say that of course when you told it
to me it was by way of an example your point being a crush is not real
not a relationship you have a crush on movie stars but you trust me with
your son your most beloved you pick me up take me out buy me wine
take me home throw me on the bed lick me like your lips are butterflies
feeding from a flower expanding as if on speeded up film or at the
bottom of my cup and then you make love to me as if i am a movie star
with a perfect body two hundred dollar a bottle portuguese wine lips
and a sweet tea blossom between her legs

the best about me

the girl with the tangled clusters of curls
and her fierce dark blue eyes
her cheeks flushed with dancing or tears
she never stops moving
cartwheels through the living room
ballet and hip hop in the garden
brazilian sea goddess combinations on the shore
escaping into movement like it's a story
where everyone is together at the end

the boy with the luxurious brown mop of hair
wide spaced green eyes like two sad seas
that strong little bouncing body
those clever hands constructing a little world
where mommies and daddies live in the same house

both of them hug as if they'll never let you go
sleep with their lips squished into pouts on pillows
eyelashes spilled on their cheeks like petals
bodies gathering up all the warmth in the room
growing mysteriously hungrily so fast
i can feel the cells expanding
when i touch their hot solid buzzing feet

the best thing about me used to be my books
and now my books have come true
taken the shape of a real house with french doors
overlooking a lawn where the children play
taken the shape of a girl in white feather wings and converse
and a naked boy doing a jig through the sprinklers
even taken the shape of a man
who is learning to love them as his own
even though they would have written it differently
so that their parents stayed together

but every day
even though it's not exactly the way they dream it
this man and i
(transformed by their demands their tears
their hands curled trustingly in ours like treasures we found
and hardly know if we deserve)
are slowly trying to become
the ones they dreamed

burned mermaid

sometimes i think about that girl with the burned legs
smiling shyly dimples as she lifted her skirt to show me
the skin ragged and rough in folds over the bone
see she said *i am a mermaid*
and i felt ashamed at the way i had attacked
again and again my own externally and relatively unmaimed body

you built a fire in a bucket on the lawn
crop circle the grass scarred
charred black
you were only trying to warm us make a party
like on those beaches in brazil
where you were the one who grilled the meat
or mixed the drinks or spun the music
and watched the girls in bikinis
politely from the corner of your eye

that was before we were so consumed by flames

both of us now with our post traumatic stress disorder
it's a wonder we are here at all
drinking beers with our friends in the garden while the children play
and the flames leap before we realize they've burned through

i may seem cold around you tonight
you may seem distant
but you know if you reach out
i will always spread my legs i will always moisten open to you
i will always kiss you back
do anything you can dream up in our bed
you can see all my metaphorical scars
what happened to that sweet burned girl
see i am a mermaid
i am not afraid

marilyn's shrine and your name

i want you to look at me the way all those people look at marilyn
monroe's shrine in the hollywood museum
marilyn naked on red satin
the glowing wonder of her breasts
marilyn lipstick laughing over her shoulder
or gazing adoringly at arthur miller's long spectacled face
marilyn sad eyed and startled by death

her costumes are there black feather breasts
and giant fake diamonds between her legs
a gown like the thinnest layers of golden leaf
film clips where her hair is a halo and her eyes are headlights
simmering the screen
her breathy voice her adorable face like the face of the most beloved child
though she never felt like anyone's beloved child
so she had to be everyone's

you would never understand if i told you
that i want you to look at me
the way all those people look at marilyn
you would think   but she is monroe
sex goddess
the sexiest woman who ever lived
and you are my girlfriend
you are not angelina jolie
or even lindsey lohan
i may love you but i will never worship you
i will never stand before a wall of images of you
and get hard and feel like weeping
and wish i could have been there to take your photograph
and hold you and tell you
you are the most beautiful woman in the world
and tell you not to die

instead you managed to eek out the words *i love you*
for the first time in a year

after you told me that your ex-wife to whom you are still married
summoned you to her hospital bed
and told you that she wants to give her baby your name

i wanted to say to you *i can be hospitalized*
i can leave you
is that what i have to do?
to become your goddess
the one you worship
mourn for
see

fear

fear is the name of a punk band from the '80s
and the lead singer was lee ving

i went to see lee ving sing when my father was dancing with cancer
and it is better to watch fear on a stage and hear it scream at you
then to lie alone with it in your bed while your father tangos
in a hospital

fear is a goblin that sits inside of me
he is covered with boils and pustules   scars and coarse hair
he smells foul and shows his rotted teeth
he says *you look like this   you are me*
and you deserve nothing

fear is my friend's death goblin
he visits her at the gynecologist
and appears whenever anyone mentions the big c
he grabs her by the hips
and shakes her like a dog worrying a rag doll
he appears behind her in the mirror
whenever she is examining the scars at her abdomen and he says *see i'm*
real
i almost got you once
you were only thirty and thus imagined yourself invincible
i'm still here
remember

your fear is not a punk band or ugliness or cancer
it is a baby the size of your palm
kept alive only by tubes that are about to be removed

after you went to the hospital and saw your fear goblin
i thought i had lost you
you said to me *if you give me love i give you love*
if you give me fear i give you fear

fear makes me back away i don't want fear in my life
you seem very afraid
i said *if my child comes to me with fear i give her love*
if my child attacks me with fear i give him love
if someone else attacks me with fear it is harder
but if anyone comes to me with fear i try to give them love instead
and then i started to cry at our restaurant with the heat lamps
the lattice work patio strung with christmas lights
the sexy dark-haired waitresses in black jeans
the olive oil   pita bread   grapes leaves   salads   grilled meats
the hookah pipe at the next table
and you drove me to your apartment building
and finally your eyes were soft again
like wine like christmas lights in the june dark
and you said *we can make this work*
we can do whatever it takes
and you took me upstairs and made love to me
and the goblins were locked outside the door
where they could only hear our groans and screams of love
and weep

sublimation

i want the house
pale pinky yellow wood with white trim
big windows wooden floors built-ins new tile
the sweet garden with the big old tree
dressed in christmas lights the elf hut in its branches
the tiny pond the terrace

it is old and young at the same time
it is pretty but not ostentatious or flashy
it has magic
it has secrets
all of which it is willing to share if you listen

i stood and cried at the picket fence
my tears watering the roses
the wind blew through the top of my open water bottle
like my father's ghost whistling *this should be yours*
and a hummingbird came and looked into my mother's eyes
giving her the same message for me
i moved my buddha statue under the tree to look at the house
from across the street
my friend's everyday miracle beads in his lap
but two sexy teenage boys stole him away
and left a big blue shoe in his place
i caught one of them with the shoe
but by then the buddha was gone
where is my buddha statue? i asked
and the boy feigned innocence
what's a buddha? he said
i try to understand what i am to glean
from the stolen buddha
and the dream of the endangered child

my house sits across the street waiting to be purchased
by me or my rival

my house yearns for the voices of three children
the whispers of a man and a woman making love
it wants to be the place where books are written
paintings painted and music played
it wants me as much as i want it

but i have a secret
as much as i want that house
if you said to me *come and live with me in my little apartment*
with our combined three children and my cat and your dog
no room for your desk or half your clothes
i would be just as happy
i would come just as readily
i would do anything whatever it takes
this is another way my house and i are alike
she doesn't just want me
she wants you too

in my garden

your curls black and soft as those clouds of leaves in the sky above us
the green hair of the earth beneath my fingernails
i grasp her like a lover
weeping into her *i am so sorry for what we have done to you*
please forgive us

this patch of unmown lawn
the circle of our passion
verdant and hidden
blessed by the moon and hestia
the garden gurgling and whispering around us
like fairies like stone cupids and goddesses come to life
the sky full of stars like planes and stars like stars
the moon low and silver full trying to expose us
but gently

there is no denying this
she says as the beautiful ones keep dying
it is as real   if not more so   my darlings
as your loss   your fear   your grief

open letter to quiet light

Dear Quiet Light

I pointed out that quiet light was the meaning of your name. You were very proud of it. You never asked me what my name means.

In my head at night now you are a dark cacophony.

You told me *When I came to L.A. I wondered, where is the booty? It's all boobs, no booty. Where I come from we like the booty.*

I wondered if it crossed your mind as you spoke that, though strong, I am very small.

You told me *My wife had big boobs when I met her. Then she lost a lot of weight, lost the boobs. I wasn't as attracted to her after that.*

You told me *I have a crush on Lindsey Lohan. Even though she is messed up she is very pretty.*

You let me walk home alone in the dark when my son burned himself on the firecracker. You didn't call to see how we were.

You pretended you did not know me.

You ignored a hundred poems.

You never looked me in the face when we made love.

But there were sweet things. You said *I have never felt this close to anyone in my life.* (Did you look those women you felt less close to in the face?)

Every time you arrived at my door in the dark and I asked, *How are you?* you growled gently, *Better now.*

After we made love you sat so quietly on the floor of your room and captured my spirit in shadow and light. Then you were your name.

You played sweetly with my children. You sat through two hours of off key music to hear my daughter sing. You held her hand.

You called me back, after you told me that your wife wanted to give your name to the baby she was having with another man, and you said, *Hey. I love you.* Those words were not easy for you to say.

About a month later you were gone. You said, *I need my space.* You said, *I don't want a girlfriend.* You said, *I like my freedom.*
These were the caustic stings of your scorpion tail.

I hope that you never sting yourself that way. Or perhaps, as scorpions do, you already have, though you may not know it yet.

Baby, you never asked. But my name? It means
Free